The Great Tribulation

God's Final Harvest

Elwood Trost

Studio of Books LLC
5900 Balcones Drive Suite 100
Austin, Texas 78731
www.studioofbooks.org
Hotline: (254) 800-1183

Ordering Information:
Special discounts are available on quantity purchases by corporations, associations, and others. For details, contact the publisher at the address above.

Printed in the United States of America.

ISBN-13: Softcover 978-1-970283-30-3
eBook 978-1-970283-31-0

Library of Congress Control Number:

Unless otherwise indicated, Bible quotations are taken from The New King James Version.

"About the Time of the End, a body of men will be raised up who will turn their attention to the prophecies and insist on their literal interpretation in the midst of much clamor and opposition." Sir Isaac Newton

Whose voice then shook the earth; but now He has promised, saying, "Yet once more I shake not only the earth, but also heaven." Now this, "Yet once more," indicates the removal of those things that are being shaken, as of things that are made, that the things which cannot be shaken may remain. Therefore, since we are receiving a kingdom which cannot be shaken, let us have grace, by which we may serve God acceptably with reverence and godly fear. For our God is a consuming fire (Hebrews 12:26-28).

John the Baptist prophesied:

I indeed baptize you with water unto repentance, but He who is coming after me is mightier than I, whose sandals I am not worthy to carry. He will baptize you with the Holy Spirit and fire. His winnowing fan is in His hand, and He will thoroughly clean out His threshing floor, and gather His wheat into the barn; but He will burn up the chaff with unquenchable fire" (Matthew 3:11-12).

Contents

Preface

Many of the younger generation have not been exposed to any Bible teaching because the Bible is not allowed in our public schools today.

I would like to reach all generations with this book and for those who have not heard of the word rapture, It is a word that has been coined for the resurrection. The resurrection/rapture is mentioned in the following Scriptures that talks about Jesus raising His followers from the dead when He returns.

But I do not want you to be ignorant, brethren, concerning those who have fallen asleep, lest you sorrow as others who have no hope. For if we believe that Jesus died and rose again, even so God will bring with Him those who sleep in Jesus. For this we say to you by the word of the Lord, that we who are alive and remain until the coming of the Lord will by no means precede those who are asleep. For the Lord Himself will descend from heaven with a shout, with the voice of an archangel, and with the trumpet of God. And the dead in Christ will rise first. Then we who are alive and remain shall be caught up together with them in the clouds to meet the Lord in the air. And thus, we shall always be with the Lord. (I Thessalonians 4:13-17).

Notice the resurrection precedes the rapture and not the other way around. Our hope as believers should be in the resurrection and not a rapture that might not happen. The road to glory is paved with sacrifice and suffering. It is the refiners fire.

Behold, I tell you a mystery: We shall not all sleep, but we shall all be changed in a moment, in the twinkling of an eye, at the last trumpet. For the trumpet will sound, and the dead will be raised incorruptible, and we shall be changed (I Corinthians 15:51-52).

The Bible teaches when Jesus returns there will be a resurrection of those who have put their faith and trust in Him.

The unbelievers (those who have rejected the gospel of Jesus Christ) will be resurrected, but they have a different destination and will spend eternity in what the bible calls the lake of fire and separated from God.

One more concept that the younger generation may have never heard of is the tribulation that closes out this age and brings in the millennial reign of Christ. It is referred to as Daniel's 70th Week, which is a seven-year period divided into two 3½ years periods. The first half referred to by Jesus as the "beginning of sorrows" and the last 3½ years as the Great Tribulation with Jesus returning and defeating the Antichrist and his armies at the end of it.

My purpose is to help you understand the end-time prophecies and what God's purposes are during this time. It will be a very difficult time for all of us but very rewarding for the believers. It is important to know the truth to make it through these hard times. I believe we need to prepare for this time now because it is at the door.

God's harvest time is the tribulation, and He wants His people here to help bring in the harvest. Jesus told His disciples to pray that God would send laborers into the harvest.

INTRODUCTION

As I have worked on this book over the last couple of years, the Lord has opened my understanding that the coming tribulation is not only an evil and negative event, but that it will be a glorious and powerful time for the followers and believers in Jesus.

I believe the true believers will be unified during the persecution that Jesus tells will come to all nations. And when unified they will receive more power that so many desire and are praying for. The people of God will be doing great exploits during this time.

This will be a fulfillment of Jesus' words that those that follow Him will do greater works than He did. The bride will go through a preparation time to meet her groom (Jesus), because He is coming back for a bride without spot or wrinkle. This time of the Great Tribulation is God's refining fire to get us ready to meet Him.

And I heard, as it were, the voice of a great multitude, as the sound of many waters and as the sound of mighty thunderings, saying, "Alleluia! For the Lord God Omnipotent reigns! Let us be glad and rejoice and give Him glory, for the marriage of the Lamb has come, and His wife has made herself ready." And to her it was granted to be arrayed in fine linen, clean and bright, for the fine linen is the righteous acts of the saints (Revelation19:6-8).

The scroll we read about in chapter five of Revelation is the title deed to the earth and only the Lamb of God, Who is Jesus, is qualified to open it.

The seals will be opened in the last seven years of this age. We will see a multitude of souls saved during this time because of the judgments of God are redemptive and this is God's harvest time. In a closer of study of Revelation, I will show that it is only the last year of the seven years that is God's wrath. The first six years are God's judgments that are redemptive

For when Your judgments are in the earth, the inhabitants of the world

will learn righteousness (Isaiah 26:9).

After these things I looked, and behold, a great multitude which no one could number, of all nations, tribes, peoples, and tongues, standing before the throne and before the Lamb, clothed with white robes, with palm branches in their hands (Revelation 7:9).

Then one of the elders answered, saying to me, "Who are these arrayed in white robes, and where did they come from?" And I said to him, "Sir, you know." So, he said to me, "These are the ones who come out of the great tribulation and washed their robes and made them white in the blood of the Lamb. Therefore, they are before the throne of God and serve Him day and night in His temple. And He who sits on the throne will dwell among them. They shall neither hunger anymore nor thirst anymore; the sun shall not strike them, nor any heat; for the Lamb who is in the midst of the throne will shepherd them and lead them to living fountains of waters. And God will wipe away every tear from their eyes." (Revelation 7:13-17).

From these verses we can see that the Great Tribulation is God's plan to bring in the harvest and to rid the earth of sin and evil by His purifying fire:

See that you do not refuse Him who speaks. For if they did not escape who refused Him who spoke on earth, much more shall we not escape if we turn away from Him who speaks from heaven, whose voice then shook the earth; but now He has promised, saying, "Yet once more I shake not only the earth, but also heaven." Now this, "Yet once more," indicates the removal of those things that are being shaken, as of things that are made, that the things which cannot be shaken may remain. Therefore, since we are receiving a kingdom which cannot be shaken, let us have grace, by which we may serve God acceptably with reverence and godly fear. For our God is a consuming fire (Hebrews 12:25-29).

It is time to prepare for what is coming by working on our relationship with Jesus. This will require spending more time in His Word and prayer. Also, fasting will be needed because of the intensity of what we will be experiencing as God closes out this age. This is a time to repent and forsake our sins to receive the power to stand. We will need to get to know the comfort of the Comforter, which is Holy Spirit, to help us get through the hard times we will be experiencing.

The Antichrist is soon to come. We know from Scripture it will be the worst time in human history, but to offset this, we know the good news is God will use these events to remove wickedness from the earth and set up His kingdom.

If you study end-time prophecy and put it together piece by piece like a puzzle, you can get a clear picture of the end-times. You don't have to be a Bible scholar to understand it, but you need "to study to show ourselves approved. God has given us 150 chapters in the Bible concerning the second coming of Christ and the time we are in. If you will pray and ask God to lead you in your study, we will be able to comprehend it.

If you learn the end-time prophecies, you will be able to recognize the Antichrist when he comes and have confidence when the judgments fall. Many who don't understand what God is doing will be offended and turn away from God. The bible predicts a great falling away in this time of testing and if you are not prepared you could be one of them.

And let's remember the encouragement that Jesus and apostle Paul have given us:

Blessed are those who are persecuted for righteousness' sake, for theirs is the kingdom of heaven. "Blessed are you when they revile and persecute you and say all kinds of evil against you falsely for My sake. Rejoice and be exceedingly glad, for great is your reward in heaven, for so they persecuted the prophets who were before you (Matthew 5:10-12).

And:

Therefore, we do not lose heart. Even though our outward man is perishing, yet the inward man is being renewed day by day. For our light affliction, which is for a moment, is working for us a far more exceeding and eternal weight of glory"- (II Corinthians 4:17).

Let's not fear what is coming and meet it with faith and the power of God and let's remain in His peace, joy, and be at rest while we go through this time of testing.

Now let's get started on putting our end-time prophecy together…

Chapter 1

DANIEL'S 70th WEEK

I will start with an explanation of how we know this age ends in a seven-year tribulation which is referred to as Daniel's 70th week. It is the backbone of end-time prophecy and gives us an outline and a road map to the second coming of Jesus.

"Seventy weeks are determined for your people and for your holy city, to finish the transgression, to make an end of sins, to make reconciliation for iniquity, to bring in everlasting righteousness, to seal up vision and prophecy, and to anoint the Most Holy. (Daniel 9:24)

Seventy weeks is seventy weeks of years or 490 years of which 483 years have been fulfilled, leaving seven years to be fulfilled at the end of this age.

This is a time when God will finish the transgression, and make an end of sins, making reconciliation for iniquity, and bring in everlasting righteousness, sealing up vision and prophecy, and anointing the Most Holy.

"Know therefore and understand, that from the going forth of the command to restore and build Jerusalem until Messiah the Prince, there shall be seven weeks and sixty-two weeks; the street shall be built again, and the wall, even in troublesome times (Daniel 9:25).

"And after the sixty-two weeks Messiah shall be cut off, but not for Himself; and the people of the prince who is to come shall destroy the city

and the sanctuary. The end of it shall be with a flood, and till the end of the war desolations are determined (Daniel 9:26).

In verses 26 and 27, we see 69 weeks of the 70 weeks of this prophecy are divided into two parts. So, these verses claim that there will be seven weeks (49 years), from the command to restore and build Jerusalem and until the covenant renewal and 62 weeks (434 years), from the covenant renewal until Messiah will be cut off.

This was fulfilled to the day by our Lord's crucifixion. Then in 70 A.D. the sanctuary was destroyed fulfilling the rest of this prophecy.

Then, there is a 2,000-year intermission between verses 26 and 27 and then in verse 27, we see Daniel's 70th week will be fulfilled in our day.

Then he shall confirm a covenant with many for one week (seven years); but in the middle of the week he shall bring an end to sacrifice and offerings;and on the wing of abominations shall be one who makes desolate, even until the consummation, which is determined, is poured out on the desolate" (Daniel 9:27).

Halfway through the seven years at the 3½ year mark the Antichrist breaks this peace treaty and invades Israel. He will sit in the temple of God and claim to be God. He will take away the daily sacrifices and demand worship. This will begin the Great Tribulation that will last the last half and remaining 3½ years.

Jesus referred to it as the "abomination of desolation," and mentions it halfway through the signs He gave us about His second coming. (Matthew 24:15).

Chapter twelve of Revelation is in the context of the Great Tribulation and gives a glimpse of what the people of God will be doing during the reign of the Antichrist:

And war broke out in heaven: Michael and his angels fought with the dragon; and the dragon and his angels fought, but they did not prevail, nor was a place found for them in heaven any longer. So, the great dragon was cast out, that serpent of old, called the Devil and Satan, who deceives the whole world; he was cast to the earth, and his angels were cast out with him.

Then I heard a loud voice saying in heaven, "Now salvation, and strength, and the kingdom of our God, and the power of His Christ have come, for the accuser of our brethren, who accused them before our God day and night, has been cast down. And they overcame him by the blood of the Lamb and by the word of their testimony, and they did not love their lives to the death. Therefore rejoice, O heavens, and you who dwell in them! Woe to the inhabitants of the earth and the sea! For the devil has come down to you, having great wrath, because he knows that he has a short time." (Revelation 12:7-12).

Satan is cast down to the earth, and he possesses the Antichrist. He knows his time is short and it says woe to the inhabitants of the earth; this short time is the 3½ years of the Great Tribulation.

But notice what is said about the people of God during this same time. Salvation and strength and power have come and they overcame him, by the blood of the Lamb, the world of their testimony, and loved not their lives to the death.

Yes, the Antichrist has some of God's people martyred but that defeats him and seals his doom gives a righteous God the right to cast him into the lake of fire.

Jesus defeated Satan when He went to the cross and His followers get the privilege in defeating the Antichrist by going to their cross during the Great Tribulation.

The Antichrist and False Prophet are thrown into the lake of fire when Jesus returns, and Satan is bound for the next 1,000 years.

All who were deceived in giving their allegiance to the Antichrist by taking the mark of the beast, are killed upon the return of Jesus:

And I saw the beast, the kings of the earth, and their armies, gathered together to make war against Him who sat on the horse and against His army. Then the beast was captured, and with him the false prophet who worked signs in his presence, by which he deceived those who received the mark of the beast and those who worshipped his image. These two were cast alive into the lake of fire burning with brimstone. And the rest were killed with the sword which proceeded from the mouth of Him who sat on the horse. And all the birds were filled with their flesh (Revelation 19:19-21).

Notice those who received the mark of the beast were deceived into taking it. The Antichrist will be a smooth talker and will deceive many. He will seem to have the answers to the world's problems and by taking his mark we will not be standing in the way of making the world a better place. But if we take his mark, we will be giving our allegiance to Satan without the possibility of repenting of our sins and being saved if we take his mark.

We need to know end- time prophecy so we will not be one of these that will be deceived. Those who resist taking the mark will be seen as standing in the way of progress and we will be persecuted, and we will need faith because we will not be able to buy or sell anything during the last 3½ years.

Some additional Scriptures that provide more information about the Antichrist and his objectives are:

He shall speak pompous words against the Most High, shall persecute the saints of the Most High, and shall intend to change times and law. Then the saints shall be given into his hand for a time and times and half a time (3½ years) (Daniel 7:25).

And he was given a mouth speaking great things and blasphemies, and he was given authority to continue for forty-two months (3½ years). Then he opened his mouth in blasphemy against God, to blaspheme His name, His tabernacle, and those who dwell in heaven. It was granted to him to make war with the saints and to overcome them and authority was given him over every tribe, tongue, and nation. All who dwell on the earth will worship him, whose names have not been written in the Book of Life of the Lamb slain from the foundation of the world(Revelation 13:5-8).

Some Scriptures in Isaiah that refer to the Antichrist are:

Those who see you will gaze at you, and consider you, saying: "Is this the man who made the earth tremble, who shook kingdoms who made the world as a wilderness and destroyed its cities, who did not open the house of his prisoners?" (Isaiah 14:16-17).

Something to think about: God is a just God, and yet He allowed the first century Christians to be persecuted. They were not "appointed to wrath" and this persecution tested their faith and separated the true believers from the false believers. In other words, this persecution separated the wheat from the chaff. It seems inconsistent if God would allow the last century Christians to be whisked away and miss a chance for their faith to be tested.

In conclusion, seventy weeks of years were given to us prophetically by Daniel of which sixty-nine weeks have been fulfilled, leaving one week that has not been fulfilled. A covenant will be confirmed with many for one week that will begin the final seven years of this age. Halfway through the seven years the Antichrist will break the covenant and invade Israel. He will proclaim himself to be God and demand to be worshipped. This will cause the great apostasy of many who claim to be Christians to fall away from the faith. The ones who don't understand what is happening will be deceived and take the mark of the beast. Also, they will be offended at God because of their lack of understanding and what God is doing.

The false prophet brings down fire from heaven and performs signs and wonders to deceive many people. Everyone whose name is not written in the Lamb's Book of Life will worship the image of the beast. (Revelation 13:8).

The Antichrist will be credited with making the earth tremble, making it a wilderness, and destroying all the cities of the world. The believers will be made ready for the resurrection by following in the footsteps of Jesus and experiencing the "fellowship of His sufferings." During this time the church will experience revival and see the fulfilment of Jesus' words that "we will do greater works" than He did. There will be a massive harvest of souls into His kingdom.

And this gospel of the kingdom will be preached in all the world as a witness to all the nations, and then the end will come (Matthew 24:14).

The good news is our Lord will use these end-time events to bring this present world system to an end and refine and deliver His people.

If you have never accepted Jesus as your Lord and Savior, this would be a very good day to do so. The end of days is upon us, and as for tomorrow, there are no guarantees. Those who have accepted Jesus will experience everlasting life and those who have not accepted God's gift of salvation will experience shame and condemnation without the possibility of changing because of what we read in Revelation:

"He who is unjust, let him be unjust still; he who is filthy, let him be filthy still; he who is righteous, let him be righteous still; he who is holy, let him be holy still" (Revelation 22:11).

Don't put it off. You will want Jesus on your side for what is coming. Let's go to the next chapter and see what the word says about the seals of the book of Revelation.

Chapter 2

THE SEALS OF REVELATION

In the book of Revelation, in chapter five we read about a scroll that is sealed with seven seals, and no one is worthy to open the seals except the Lamb of God. The scroll is the title deed to the earth and Jesus is the only one who is worthy to open it.

The scroll is a parchment that is rolled up and held closed with seals. The first seal must be broken before the scroll can be opened and unrolled and read. When you get to the next seal it needs to be broken and you can read the next part of the scroll, and so on. This translates today into something like chapters in a book. The seals are opened one after another or chronologically.

There are 21 judgments of God (three sets of seven) that are organized into seven seals, seven trumpets, and seven bowls, each getting closer together and more intense like birth-pangs. There are seven seals, and the seventh seal introduces and contains the seven trumpet judgments, and the seventh trumpet introduces and contains the seven bowl judgments.

In chapter six of Revelation, we see the seals are beginning to be opened and what they release. These seals are the same signs Jesus gave us about His second coming with more details.

1st Seal: (Deception)

Now I saw when the Lamb opened one of the seals; and I heard one of the four living creatures saying with a voice like thunder, "Come and see. And I looked, and behold, a white horse. He who sat on it had a bow; and a crown was given to him, and he went out conquering and to conquer (Revelation 6:1-2).

Jesus answered and said to them: "Take heed that no one deceives you. For many will come in My name, saying, 'I am the Christ,' and will deceive many" (Matthew 24:4-5).

There is a covenant confirmed at the opening of the first seal. It is a false peace and will not last.

2nd Seal: (War)

When He opened the second seal, I heard the second living creature saying, "Come and see." Another horse, fiery red, went out. And it was granted to the one who sat on it to take peace from the earth, and that people should kill one another; and there was given to him a great sword (Revelation 6:3-4).

And you will hear of wars and rumors of wars. See that you are not troubled; for all these things must come to pass, but the end is not yet. For nation will rise against nation, and kingdom against kingdom (Matthew 24:6-7).

The peace covenant will not last, and we will see peace taken from the earth and a great sword could be a reference of nuclear weapons being used.

But concerning the times and the seasons, brethren, you have no need that I should write to you. You yourselves know perfectly that the day of the Lord so comes as a thief in the night. For when they say, "Peace and safety!" then sudden destruction comes upon them, as labor pains upon a pregnant woman. And they shall not escape you, brethren, are not in darkness, so that this Day should overtake you as a thief are all sons of light and sons of the day. We are not of the night nor of darkness (1 Thessalonians 5:1-5).

3rd Seal: (Famine)

When He opened the third seal, I heard the third living creature say, "Come and see." So I looked, and behold, a black horse, and he who sat on it had a pair of scales in his hand. And I heard a voice in the midst of the four living creatures saying, "A quart of wheat for a denarius, and three quarts of barley for a denarius; and do not harm the oil and the wine" (Revelation 6:5-6).

And there will be famines, pestilences, and earthquakes in various places. All these are the beginning of sorrows (Matthew 24:7-8).

The third seal reveals to us that inflation will continue until it will take a day's wages to buy a loaf of bread. Most of bible prophesy is about the Middle East, so we don't know how much of the earth will be affected.

And as believers and followers of Yeshua, Jesus, we have this promise:

Behold, the eye of the Lord is on those who fear Him, on those who hope in His mercy, to deliver their soul from death, and to keep them alive in famine (Psalm 33:19.

The Lord knows the days of the upright, and their inheritance shall be forever. They shall not be ashamed in the evil time, and in the days of famine they shall be satisfied (Psalm 37:19).

4th Seal: (Pestilences)

When He opened the fourth seal, I heard the voice of the fourth living creature saying, "Come and see."8 So I looked, and behold, a pale horse. And the name of him who sat on it was Death, and Hades followed with him. And power was given to them over a fourth of the earth, to kill with sword, with hunger, with death, and by the beasts of the earth (Revelation 6:7-8).

And there will be famines, pestilences, and earthquakes in various places. All these are the beginning of sorrows (Matthew 24:7-8).

It is obvious that the seals and signs Jesus gives us are the same events. Jesus referred to the horses and their riders as "the beginning of sorrows." These horses represent how the Antichrist comes into power, and notice there is no more riders because we are now at the midpoint of the Daniel's 70th Week and the Antichrist will rule for the last half of it for next 3½ years.

Now, the world is under Antichrist's rule and the earth will experience death over one-fourth of it by the sword and hunger and the forth seal is when we will see the "abomination of desolation," set up and the beginning the Great Tribulation.

5th Seal: (Martyrdom)

When He opened the fifth seal, I saw under the altar the souls of those who had been slain for the word of God and for the testimony which they held. And they cried with a loud voice, saying, "How long, O Lord, holy and true, until You judge and avenge our blood on those who dwell on the earth?" Then a white robe was given to each of them; and it was said to them that they should rest a little while longer, until both the number of their fellow servants and their brethren, who would be killed as they were, was completed(Revelation 6:9-11).

Then they will deliver you up to tribulation and kill you, and you will be hated by all nations for My name's sake. And then many will be offended, and will betray one another, and will hate one another 11 Then many false prophets will rise up and deceive many. And because lawlessness will abound, the love of many will grow cold. But he who endures to the end shall be saved. And this gospel of the kingdom will be preached in all the world as a witness to all the nations, and then the end will come (Matthew 24:9-14).

When the fifth seal is opened, those appointed to martyrdom will be martyred. The Antichrist will demand worship and martyr those who will not worship him.

Therefore, when you see the 'abomination of desolation,' spoken of by Daniel the prophet, standing in the holy place" (whoever reads, let him understand. "Then let those who are in Judea flee to the mountains. Let him who is on the housetop not go down to take anything out his house. And let him who is in the field not go back to get his clothes but woe to those who are pregnant and to those who are nursing babies in those days and pray that your flight may not be in winter or on the Sabbath. "For then there will be great tribulation, such as has not been since the beginning of the world until this time, no, nor ever shall be. And unless those days were shortened, no flesh would be saved; but for the elect's sake those days will be shortened" (Matthew 24:15-22).

One of the main things we can do to prepare for this time is to keep our hearts soft and practice forgiving and loving others, even our enemies.

Let's examine the sixth seal and see what it reveals:

6th Seal: Cosmic Signs

I looked when He opened the sixth seal, and behold, there was a great earthquake; and the sun became black as sackcloth of hair, and the moon became like blood. And the stars of heaven fell to the earth, as a fig tree drops its late figs when it is shaken by a mighty wind. Then the sky receded as a scroll when it is rolled up, and every mountain and island was moved out of its place. And the kings of the earth, the great men, the rich men, the commanders, the mighty men, every slave and every free man, hid themselves in the caves and in the rocks of the mountains and said to the mountains and rocks, "Fall on us and hide us from the face of Him who sits on the throne and from the wrath of the Lamb! For the great day of His wrath has come, and who is able to stand?" (Revelation 6:12-17).

Cosmic signs are displayed at the opening of the sixth seal and in verse 17 we see that these signs are announcing the wrath of God is about to begin.

There are two more Scriptures in the New Testament where we see these signs that are mentioned at the opening of the sixth seal. One is in Luke, and the other one is in Matthew:

And there will be signs in the sun, in the moon, and in the stars; and on the earth distress of nations, with perplexity, the sea and the waves roaring men's hearts failing them from fear and the expectation of those things which are coming on the earth, for the powers of the heavens will be shaken. Then they will see the Son of Man coming in a cloud with power and great glory. Now when these things begin to happen, look up and lift up your heads, because your redemption draws near" (Luke 21:25-28).

The Scripture in Luke describes the cosmic signs and their message is "your redemption draws near." So far the cosmic signs tell us that the 'wrath of God" is imminent, and His second coming is near. Therefore, if we put these verses together, the cosmic signs seem to take place before the second coming but are a warning that it is coming soon.

The Scripture in Matthew reads:

Immediately after the tribulation of those days the sun will be darkened, and the moon will not give its light; the stars will fall from heaven, and the powers of the heavens will be shaken. Then the sign of the Son of Man will appear in heaven, and then all the tribes of the earth will mourn, and they will see the Son of Man coming on the clouds of heaven with power and great glory. And He will send His angels with a great sound of a trumpet, and they will gather together His elect from the four winds, from one end of heaven to the other (Matthew 24:29-31).

This Scripture describes the second coming. And if the cosmic signs in these three passages are the same events. This would mean Jesus is giving us an outline and if we put the three Scriptures together, we see there is a time delay between the signs and the second coming. This makes sense because this gives a space of time for the seventh seal to be opened and the trumpet judgments to sound. This is why we say the seals give us more detail to the signs the Jesus give us.

The seals are being opened chronologically and the seventh seal hasn't been opened yet and it contains the seven trumpets that need to sound before Jesus returns.

We know we can conclude that the Lord returns during the seventh trumpet judgment or "last trump," and not at the sixth seal.

Then the 144,000 are sealed to go through the trumpet judgments and the "wrath of God" that begins with trumpets sounding.

After these things I saw four angels standing at the four corners of the earth, holding the four winds of the earth, that the wind should not blow on the earth, on the sea, or on any tree. [2] Then I saw another angel ascending from the east, having the seal of the living God. And he cried with a loud voice to the four angels to whom it was granted to harm the earth and the sea [3] saying, "Do not harm the earth, the sea, or the trees till we have sealed the servants of our God on their foreheads. [4] And I heard the number of those who were sealed. One hundred and forty-four thousand of all the tribes of the children of Israel were sealed (Revelation 7:1-4).

After the 144,000 are sealed on their foreheads, John receives a vision of those who went through the great tribulation and those who were made ready for heaven by being refined (Revelation 7:9-17).

Seventh Seal: Prelude to the Seven Trumpets

When He opened the seventh seal, there was silence in heaven for about half an hour. And I saw the seven angels who stand before God, and to them were given /seven trumpets. Then another angel, having a golden censer, came and stood at the altar. He was given much incense, that he should offer it with the prayers of all the saints upon the golden altar which was before the throne. And the smoke of the incense, with the prayers of the saints, ascended before God from the angel's hand. Then the angel took the censer, filled it with fire from the altar, and threw it to the earth. And there were noises, thunderings, lightnings, and an earthquake. So the seven angels who had the seven trumpets prepared themselves to sound (Revelation 8-1-6).

In summary, the seals are being opened chronologically with the first four seals being opened in the first 3½ years of the of Daniel's 70th Week, leaving the last three to open during the last half.

The followers of Jesus are going through the refiner's fire and being purified to be His bride. We will see a great revival, and the great commission will be fulfilled, At the same time this world and its systems will experiencing deception, wars, famines, pestilences, earthquakes, and death.

During the fifth seal the Antichrist and his followers will persecute the Christians that resist taking his mark. But this is a blessing in disguise because it will be our transformation from these bodies that get sick and die into new bodies that God has for us that will never get sick or die again.

The sixth seal is opened with comic signs announcing that the wrath of God is getting ready to begin, and 144,000 are sealed to go through them.

Then, the seventh seal is opened, and the trumpets begin to sound and at "last trump," the Lord returns and resurrects/raptures His elect. He will deliver the bowl Judgements in person which completes the wrath of God. And then he will set up His millennial reign.

Chapter 3

THE TRUMPET JUDGMENTS

At the opening of the seventh seal the trumpet judgments begin to sound. When the seventh trumpet sounds the earth becomes the Lord's(Revelation 11:15).

Jesus Christ returns at the seventh trumpet or "last trump" and the resurrection/rapture takes place at this time.

When the trumpets begin to sound, things on planet earth will never be the same. The first six seals did not involve angels, but as the "wrath of God" begins with the trumpets, angels become involved. We should have the attitude that Job had:

Though He slay me, yet will I trust Him. Even so, I will defend my own ways before Him. He also shall be my salvation, for a hypocrite could not come before Him (Job 13:15).

Let's look at the trumpet judgments now:

1st Trumpet: Vegetation Struck

The first angel sounded: And hail and fire followed, mingled with blood, and they were thrown to the earth. And a third of the trees were burned up, and all green grass was burned up (Revelation 8:7).

These trumpets even though they are God's wrath they are tempered to allow more to come to repentance and be saved. God's will is that all come to repentance and be saved.

2nd Trumpet: Seas Struck

Then the second angel sounded: And something like a great mountain burning with fire was thrown into the sea, and a third of the sea became blood. And a third of the living creatures in the sea died, and a third of the ships were destroyed (Revelation 8:8-9).

3rd Trumpet: Waters Struck

Then the third angel sounded: And a great star fell from heaven, burning like a torch, and it fell on a third of the rivers and on the springs of water. The name of the star is Wormwood. A third of the waters became wormwood, and many men died from the water, because it was made bitter (Revelation 8:10 -11).

4th Trumpet: Heavens Struck

Then the fourth angel sounded: And a third of the sun was struck, a third of the moon, and a third of the stars, so that a third of them were darkened. A third of the day did not shine, and likewise the night. And I looked, and I heard an angel flying through the midst of heaven, saying with a loud voice, "Woe, woe, woe to the inhabitants of the earth, because of the remaining blasts of the trumpet of the three angels who are about to sound!" (Revelation 8:12-13).

5th Trumpet: Locusts from the Bottomless Pit

Then the fifth angel sounded: And I saw a star fallen from heaven to the earth. To him was given the key to the bottomless pit. And he opened the bottomless pit, and smoke arose out of the pit like the smoke of a great furnace. So, the sun and the air were darkened because of the smoke of the pit. [3] Then out of the smoke locusts came upon the earth. And to them was given power, as the scorpions of the earth have power. They were commanded not to harm the grass of the earth, or any green thing, or any tree, but only those men who do not have the seal of God on their foreheads. And they were not given authority to kill them, but to torment them for five months. Their torment was like the torment of a scorpion when it strikes a man. In those days men will seek death and will not find it; they will desire to die, and death will flee from them. The shape of the locusts was like horses prepared for battle. On their heads were crowns of something like gold, and their faces were like the faces of men. They had hair like women's hair, and their teeth were like lions' teeth. And they had breastplates like breastplates of iron, and the sound of their wings was like the sound of chariots with many horses running into battle. They had tails like scorpions, and there were stings in their tails. Their power was to hurt men five months. And they had as king over them the angel of the bottomless pit, whose name in Hebrew is Abaddon, but in Greek he has the name Apollyon. One woe is past. Behold, still two more woes are coming after these things(Revelation 9:1-12).

We can see that things are getting rough for those who have rejected the Lord and chose to serve the Antichrist.

The 144,000 have been sealed to go through the trumpet judgments while the woman of Revelation chapter twelve, which is made up of all the other believers in the Jewish Messiah Jesus, are being protected in a place in the wilderness that God has prepared for her to be fed and protected for 1260 days, time, times, and half a time. These 3½ years of the Great Tribulation include the trumpets that sound the last year. (Revelation 12:6; 12:13-14).

I believe the 144,000 are proclaiming "the day of vengeance of our God." (Isaiah 61:2b) Jesus quoted Isaiah 61:2 and stopped in the middle of this verse because He knew that this day of vengeance was 2,000 years in the future.

Multitudes are in the valley of decision at this time. God in His mercy and grace is still saving those who will repent and call on His name. This chance for someone to be saved is drawing to the close though.

Multitudes, multitudes in the valley of decision! For the day of the Lord is near in the valley of decision. The sun and moon will grow dark, and the stars will diminish their brightness. The Lord also will roar from Zion and utter His voice from Jerusalem; The heavens and earth will shake; But the Lord will be a shelter for His people, and the strength of the children of Israel (Joel 3:14-16).

6th Trumpet: The Angels from the Euphrates

Then the sixth angel sounded: And I heard a voice from the four horns of the golden altar which is before God saying to the sixth angel who had the trumpet, release the four angels who are bound at the great river Euphrates. So, the four angels, who had been prepared for the hour and day and month and year, were released to kill a third of mankind. Now the number of the army of the horsemen was two hundred million; I heard the number of them. And thus I saw the horses in the vision: those who sat on them had breastplates of fiery red, hyacinth blue, and sulfur yellow; and the heads of the horses were like the heads of lions; and out of their mouths came fire, smoke, and brimstone. By these three plagues a third of mankind was killed-by the fire and the smoke and the brimstone which came out of their mouths. For their power is in their mouth and in their tails; for their tails are like serpents, having heads; and with them they do harm. But the rest of mankind, who were not killed by these plagues, did not repent of the works of their hands, that they should not worship demons, and idols of gold, silver, brass, stone, and wood, which can neither see nor hear nor walk. And they did not repent of their murders or their sorceries or their sexual immorality or their thefts (Revelation 9:13-21).

Time has run out for people to be saved. Those who have taken the mark of the beast cannot repent now to be saved and they are doomed for eternity.

7th Trumpet: The Lord Returns and the Kingdom Proclaimed

The seventh angel sounded: And there were loud voices in heaven saying, "The kingdoms of this world have become the kingdoms of our Lord and of His Christ, and He shall reign forever and ever!" And the twenty-four elders who sat before God on their thrones fell on their faces and worshipped God, saying: We give You thanks, O Lord God Almighty, The One who is and who was, and who is to come, Because You have taken Your great power and reigned. The nations were angry, and Your wrath has come, And the time of the dead, that they should be judged, and that You should reward Your servants the prophets and the saints, and those who fear Your name, small and great, and should destroy those who destroy the earth. Then the temple of God was opened in heaven, and the ark of His covenant was seen in His temple. And there were lightnings, noises, thunderings, an earthquake, and great hail (Revelation 11:15-19).

Let's bring this all together: The seals have been opened, and when the seventh seal was opened the trumpets begin to sound and the 144,000 go out proclaiming that "the day of vengeance of our God," is here.

God in His mercy has tempered the trumpets to give more time for people to repent and be saved. Then, the sign of the Son of Man appears at the "last trump," and we see Jesus coming through the clouds. He resurrects and raptures His remnant, and they become His mighty army. Then He treads "the wine press of the wrath of God" Himself which are the bowl judgments:

Now I saw heaven opened, and behold, a white horse. And He who sat on him was called Faithful and True, and in righteousness He judges and makes war. His eyes were like a flame of fire, and on His head were many crowns. He had a name written that no one knew except Himself. He was clothed with a robe dipped in blood, and His name is called The word of God. And the armies in heaven, clothed in fine linen, white and clean, followed Him on white horses. Now out of His mouth goes a sharp sword, that with it He should strike the nations. And He Himself will rule them with a rod of iron. He Himself treads the winepress of the fierceness and wrath of Almighty God. And He has on His robe and on His thigh a name written:

KING OF KINGS AND LORD OF LORDS (Revelation 19:11-16).

Chapter 4

THE BOWL JUDGMENTS

Come, my people, enter your chambers, and shut your doors behind you; Hide yourself, as it were, for a little moment, until the indignation is past For behold, the Lord comes out of His place to punish the inhabitants of the earth for their iniquity; the earth will also disclose her blood, and will no more cover her slain (Isaiah 26 20-21).

The book of Revelation is the revelation of Jesus Christ. He came for the first time as a lamb. He is coming the second time as a lion. He came for the first time as the Savior. He is coming back as a judge. The bowl judgments are the same events known "the great winepress of the wrath of God" (Revelation 14:19). They are a manifestation of hell coming to earth.

Jesus is forgiving and merciful to those who have accepted Him, but He is a God of vengeance for those who have rejected Him:

Kiss the Son, lest He be angry, and you perish in the way, when His wrath is kindled but a little. Blessed are those who put their trust in Him (Psalm 2:12).

The bowl judgments are very severe and because of their severity, they are shortened to only a few days or no flesh would be saved.

Sadly, however, there are those who blaspheme God right up to the very end. God's will is that no one should perish but that all would come to repentance, believe, and be Saved (II Peter 3:9).

Then I saw another sign in heaven, great and marvelous: seven angels having the seven last plagues, for in them the wrath of God is complete (Revelation 15:1).

God uses the least severe means possible to get as many as He can to repent and turn to him and receive His love without violating our freewill. He is destroying the Antichrist's system and saving all those who will come to Him. The earth will be full of murder, sorceries, immorality, and theft at this time as in the days of Noah. God is going to put an end to this so we can live in peace on earth.

1st Bowl: Loathsome Sores

The first angel went and poured out his bowl upon the earth, and a foul and loathsome sore came upon the men who had the mark of the beast and those who worshipped his image (Revelation 16:2).

2nd Bowl: Sea Turns to Blood

The second angel poured out his bowl on the sea, and it became blood as of a dead man; and every living creature in the sea died (Revelation 16:3).

3rd Bowl: Waters Turn to Blood

The third angel poured out his bowl on the rivers and springs of water, and they became blood. And I heard the angel of the waters saying: "You are righteous, O Lord, the One who is and who was and who is to be, because You have judged these things. For they have shed the blood of saints and prophets, and You have given them blood to drink. For it is their just due." I heard another from the altar saying, "Even so, Lord God Almighty" (Revelation 16:4-7).

The Antichrist has martyred many Christians not realizing he was causing his own doom. Yet the saints defeat the Antichrist by the blood of Jesus, the word of their testimony, and they loved not their lives unto death (Revelation 12:11). The saints defeat the Antichrist by laying their lives down, not trying to save them.

Jesus also said, "For whoever desires to save his life will lose it, but whoever loses his life for My sake will find it (Matthew 16:25).

4th Bowl: Men are Scorched

The fourth angel poured out his bowl on the sun, and power was given to him to scorch men with fire. Men were scorched with great heat, and they blasphemed the name of God who has power over these plagues; and they did not repent and give Him glory (Revelation 16:8-9).

5th Bowl: Darkness and Pain

The fifth angel poured out his bowl on the throne of the beast, and his kingdom became full of darkness; and they gnawed their tongues because of the pain. They blasphemed the God of heaven because of their pains and their sores and did not repent of their deeds(Revelation 16:10-11).

6th Bowl: Euphrates Dried Up

The sixth angel poured out his bowl on the great river Euphrates, and its water was dried up, so that the way of the kings from the east might be prepared. And I saw three unclean spirits like frogs coming out of the mouth of the dragon, out of the mouth of the beast, and out of the mouth of the false prophet. For they are spirits of demons, performing signs, which go out to the kings of the earth and of the whole world, to gather them to the battle of that great day of God Almighty. "Behold, I am coming as a thief. Blessed is he who watches, and keeps his garments, lest he walk naked and they see his shame." And they gathered them together to the place called in Hebrew, Armageddon (Revelation 16:12-16)

Jesus has returned at the "last trump." He is here leading a military campaign up through Jordan on His way to Jerusalem. (Isaiah 63:1-6). The kings of the east come and surround Jerusalem thinking they can defeat Him. But when Jesus reaches of the Mount of Olives, He speaks one word, and it is all over except for the shouting.

7th Bowl: The Earth Utterly Shaken

The last and seventh angel poured out his bowl into the air, and a loud voice came out of the temple of heaven, from the throne, saying, "It is done!" And there were noises and thunderings and lightnings; and there was a great earthquake, such a mighty and great earthquake as had not occurred since men were on the earth. Now the great city was divided into three parts, and the cities of the nations fell. And great Babylon was remembered before God, to give her the cup of the wine of the fierceness of His wrath. Then every island fled away, and the mountains were not found. And great hail from heaven fell upon men, each hailstone about the weight of a talent. Men blasphemed God because of the plague of the hail, since that plague was exceedingly great(Revelation 16:17-20).

Babylon means confusion and it is a symbolic reference of this present world system which is totally out of will of God. It calls good evil and evil good. When the seventh bowl is poured out, all the cities of the world fall and hailstones weighing up to 100 pounds destroy what is left. Then, Armageddon takes place and God's wrath will be complete. At this point in time, the seals, trumpets, and bowls have all been fulfilled as prophesied by John. The destruction of both religious and economic Babylon has been accomplished, making room for the kingdoms of our Lord to be established.

After these things I saw another angel coming down from heaven, having great authority, and the earth was illuminated with his glory. And he cried mightily with a loud voice, saying, "Babylon the great is fallen, is fallen, and has become a dwelling place of demons, a prison for every foul spirit, and a cage for every unclean and hated bird! For all the nations have drunk of the wine of the wrath of her fornication, the kings of the earth have committed fornication with her, and the merchants of the earth have become rich through the abundance of her luxury." And I heard another voice from heaven saying, "Come out of her, my people, lest you share in her sins, and lest you receive of her plagues. For her sins have reached to heaven, and God has remembered her iniquities. Render to her just as she rendered to you, and repay her double according to her works in the cup which she has mixed, mix double for her. In the measure that she glorified herself and lived luxuriously, in the same measure give her torment and sorrow; for she says in her heart, 'I sit as queen, and am no widow, and will not see sorrow. 'Therefore her plagues will come in one day—death and mourning and famine. And she will be utterly burned with fire, for strong is the Lord God who judges her (Revelation 18:1-8).

These chapters we have just concluded are God's battle plan to return His Son and put Him on David's throne and He will rule forever.

It is my prayer that you will take this warning seriously about what is soon to come upon believers and unbelievers alike. It is time to examine our hearts to see if we are in the faith. Prepare now and become strong enough spiritually to make it through the difficult times that lie ahead!

Satan will be bound, and we will have peace and joy for the next 1,000 years and on into eternity.

Chapter 5

TYPES AND SHADOWS

A type or shadow is an event that speaks to or gives interpretation to a future event, a foretelling. In other words, it is an event that is prophetic in nature.

One day while in prayer, I asked the Lord, how do the seals, trumpets, and bowls of Revelation relate to one another. What I heard in my heart was, "Look at my instructions to Joshua for the battle of Jericho. This is not the answer I was expecting but when I did, and if a day equals a year, I saw something very interesting.

God's instructions to Joshua are found in Joshua 6:1-5. They were to march around Jericho for seven days. Daniel's 70th Week is seven years then these seven days are a type of seals and one being opened each year. On the seventh day they were commanded to march around Jericho seven times blowing trumpets. This is a type of the trumpet judgments. Then, when the last trumpet sounded, they were to shout and the walls of the city would fall down. This is a type of the return of our Lord Jesus and the fall of the Antichrist.

Jesus returns at the "last trump" and with the "shout of an archangel" (I Thessalonians 4:16; I Corinthians 15:52).

Rahab and her household being protected is a type of the faithful being protected and then resurrected and raptured at the second coming.

Jericho being destroyed is a type of the bowls and Jesus treading out the "wine press of the wrath of God after His return ending with Armageddon.

Some other types and shadows are:

Pharaoh is a type of the Antichrist, and Moses and Aaron are types of the two prophets mentioned in chapter 11 of Revelation. God's people will be protected from the plagues like the Israelites were during the events leading up to the Exodus from Egypt. (Exodus chapters 7-14).

The Hebrew children who would not bow down and worship Nebuchadnezzar and were thrown into the fiery furnace but not burned because the fourth man (Jesus) was with them is a type of the faithful not bowing down to the Antichrist and going through the Great Tribulation being protected by Christ and His angels (Daniel 3:21-25).

Daniel in the lion's den is a type of the church who will not accept the mark of the beast, being protected during the Great Tribulation, and Daniel's adversaries being devoured is a type of what happens to the wicked when the lion of the tribe of Judah appears at the second coming (Daniel 6:10-28).

Noah's ark serves as a type of the church being protected as God's wrath is poured out. They rode above the storm but never left the earth. It is interesting that from the time the rain started, and when they stepped back on the ground was one year and ten days. (Genesis chapters 7:10-12; 8:14-15). I have the trumpets sounding one year and the bowls last ten days. I will explain where I get the ten days in my chapter on the feasts of the Lord.

In the New Testament:

Paul and Silas were beaten and thrown into jail at midnight. As they were praying and praising God, there was a great earthquake and the doors of the prison opened, and their chains fell off, and the jailer was saved. This is a type of the people of God walking in power and bringing a multitude into the kingdom of God during the Great Tribulation (Acts 16:25-26).

Paul's shipwreck, recorded in chapter 27 of Acts, the crew was trying to escape is the type of those who want to go out in the Pre-Trib Rapture. Paul said to the Romans, "Unless these men stay on board this ship, you cannot be saved." It is time to get our eyes off ourselves and how we can escape what is coming and put our attention on those who don't know Christ and are on their way to hell. We are going have a great harvest of souls during Daniel's 70th week. We need all our Christian brothers and sisters to stay on board because we are expecting a harvest of over one billion souls, and we will be needed to help bring in the harvest.

We do not have to fear, when our God is near. The Scriptures promise us God will not give more than we can bear. He will give us the grace to get through times of persecution. We just need to keep our eyes on Jesus, the author and finisher of our faith (Hebrews 12:1-2).

God is our refuge and strength, a very present help in trouble. Therefore, we will not fear, Even though the earth be removed, And though the mountains be carried into the midst of the sea; Though its waters roar and be troubled, Though the mountains shake with its swelling. There is a river whose streams shall make glad the city of God, The holy place of the tabernacle of the Most High. God is in the midst of her, she shall not be moved; God shall help her, just at the break of dawn. 6 The nations raged, the kingdoms were moved; He uttered His voice, the earth melted. The Lord of hosts is with us; The God of Jacob is our refuge. Come, behold the works of the Lord, Who has made desolations in the earth. He makes wars cease to the end of the earth; He breaks the bow and cuts the spear in two; He burns the chariot in the fire. Be still, and know that I am God; I will be exalted among the nations, I will be exalted in the earth! The Lord of hosts is with us; The God of Jacob is our refuge. Selah (Psalm 46:1-11).

Chapter 6

THE PASSION WEEK

Jesus' last seven days from the time Jesus entered Jerusalem and was crucified and raised from the dead is known as the "Passion Week." I believe it is a type or shadow of the church going through the tribulation and following in the footsteps of Jesus. If this is true, the church will have the same power Jesus had and we will fulfill Jesus' words, "That we would do greater works than He did." After this the church will follow Jesus to the cross. I believe we can get some precious insights by looking at this week. And again, seeing one day equaling a year.

My hope is that Christians can see the opportunity that going through the Great Tribulation affords them. I realize this takes a renewing of our minds. However, this time is an opportunity to show our love of God in a way we will not be able to at any other time in history. When we are heaven and everything is perfect, we will not have this opportunity ever again.

Jesus' last week: Days are from sundown to sundown.

1st day - Saturday night to Sunday, Passover lamb chosen.	Jesus enters Jerusalem on donkey and cleanses the Temple.
2nd day - Sunday night, Monday.	Lodged at Bethany. Jesus heals the blind and lame.

3rd day - Monday night, Tuesday.	Jesus teaches in the temple. Jesus gives us the signs of His second coming. Jesus warns about "abomination of desolation." Jesus warns about the world's hatred. Jesus prays for future believers to be protected not for their escape. Preparation for the Passover Supper.
4th day - Tuesday night, Wednesday.	Jesus eats Passover or "Last Supper." Gethsemane. Judas betrays Jesus. Night trial before Sanhedrin. Day trial before Sanhedrin. Peter denies knowing Jesus. From Pilate to Herod and back to Pilate again. Jesus on the cross from 9 a.m. to 3 p.m.
5th day - Wednesday night, Thursday.	Jesus buried before sundown. Feast of Unleavened bread begins. Jesus in the tomb while soldiers guard Him.
6th day - Thursday night, Friday. 1st day in the grave.	Jesus in tomb 1st day and night. Jesus in tomb on High Holy Day or Sabbath.
7th day - Friday night, Saturday. 2nd day in the grave.	Jesus in tomb 2nd day and night. Roman soldiers guarding the tomb.
Saturday night, 3rd day in the grave. Sunday morning grave is empty	Jesus in tomb 3rd day and night. Jesus resurrects from the dead before daylight.

Day 1-Saturday night to Sunday. Jesus rides into Jerusalem and cleanses Temple which is a type of Jesus cleansing the church to prepare it for tribulation.

Day 2- Sunday night to Monday. First year of the tribulation as Jesus is bringing truth to believers which brings revival and God will be releasing power to us to heal the sick, cast out demons, and raise the dead.

Day 3-Monday night to Tuesday. In the second-year multitudes are being saved. Christians will start outnumbering non-believers, and non-believers will start hating and persecuting Christians.

Day 4-Tuesday night and Wednesday. In the third-year revival continues with the great commission being fulfilled. Judas is a type of the falling away of many who take the mark of the beast to buy and sell for the next 3½ years. Antichrist is sitting in the temple and whoever will not worship him will either be put in prison or martyred.

Day 5-Wednesday night to Thursday. The fourth year the Antichrist is given power over the saints for the last 3½ years (Daniel 7:25, Revelation 13:7). However, the saints overcome him with the blood of the Lamb, the word of their testimony, and they loved not their lives to the death (Revelation 12:11).

Jesus had to be crucified and buried by Wednesday to be in the grave three full nights and days and to be resurrected on Saturday night and for the grave to be empty Sunday Morning. Jesus was put in tomb before sunset Wednesday night just before the High Holy Day began which was Unleavened Bread.

Day 6-Thursday night to Friday. Jesus in the grave 24 hours.

Day 7-Friday night to Saturday. Jesus in grave 48 hours. Jesus preaches to the disobedient spirits from the days of Noah (I Peter 3:19-20). The 144,000 are preaching to those who have failed to accept Jesus before now. This really shows the grace of God and how far He goes to redeem the lost. God is giving people their last chance to repent.

Day 1 of next week-Saturday night to Sunday. Jesus in the grave 72 hours by Saturday night. Jesus resurrects from the grave which is a type of the resurrection of the believers. Jesus returns drinks wine with us at celebration of the "marriage supper of the Lamb." Don't miss it because the real party is in heaven not in hell and heaven is coming to earth. God's plan is to dwell His people forever on the earth.

Chapter 7

THE FEASTS OF THE LORD

Spring Feasts: Fulfilled at the first coming of Jesus

Feast of Passover	Nissan 14	Leviticus 23:4-5	Fulfilled by Christ the Lamb of God on the cross
Feast of Unleavened Bread	Nissan 15	Leviticus 23:6-8	Fulfilled by Christ by living a sinless life
Feast of First Fruits	First day after the Sabbath	Leviticus 23:9-14	Fulfilled by Christ by His resurrection

Fifty days after Feast of First Fruits

Feast of Weeks or Pentecost	Fifty days after Feast of First Fruits	Leviticus 23:15-22	Fulfilled on the Day of Pentecost

Fall Feasts: Six months after Spring Feasts to be fulfilled at the second coming

Feast of Trumpets	Tishri 1	Leviticus 23:23-25	Jesus Returns at the Last Trump
Day of Atonement	Tishri 10	Leviticus 23:26-32	Armageddon
Feast of Tabernacles, Feast of Ingathering	Tishri 15	Leviticus 23:33-35	Marriage Super of the Lamb

We know that Jesus fulfilled the spring feasts of the Lord to the day and hour at His first coming and He will fulfill the fall feasts at His second coming.

Jesus was crucified on Passover, buried on Unleavened Bread, and resurrection on the feast of First fruits.

Fifty days later, the Holy Spirit was poured on the new believers on Pentecost, then we have summertime which represents the time we are in now, leaving the fall feast to be fulfilled at the second coming.

The fall feasts are the Feast of Trumpets, the Day of Atonement, and the Feast of Tabernacles.

Jesus will return on the Feast of Trumpets on the first day of Tishri (Tishri 1) to the land of Egypt as the greater Moses:

The burden against Egypt. Behold, the Lord rides on a swift cloud and will come into Egypt; The idols of Egypt will totter at His presence, and the heart of Egypt will melt in its midst. "I will set Egyptians against Egyptians; Everyone will fight against his brother, And everyone against his neighbour, City against city, kingdom against kingdom" (Isaiah 19:1-2).

Jesus will then lead a military campaign up through Jordan to the Mount of Olives, and on Tishri 10, He will reach the Mount of Olives on the Day of Atonement and Armageddon is fulfilled. (Isaiah 63:1-6; Habakkuk 3:1-16; Zackariah 14:3-4).

Jesus's army will be made up of those He resurrects at the second coming. This army is described in the book of Psalms:

For the Lord takes pleasure in His people; He will beautify the humble with salvation. Let the saints be joyful in glory; Let them sing aloud on their beds. Let the high praises of God be in their mouth, and a two-edged sword in their hand, to execute vengeance on the nations, and punishments on the peoples; To bind their kings with chains, and their nobles with fetters of iron; To execute on them the written judgment—This honor have all His saints. Praise the Lord! (Psalm 149:4-9).

Five days later, on Tishri 15, the marriage supper of the Lamb will begin. We will be celebrating Jesus with food and wine here on earth.

It is interesting that the Feast of Trumpets is referred to in Jerusalem as the feast that no one knows the day or hour. The reason for this is it is the only feast that begins on the first day of the month. This is why they set two days aside for it to start. The new moon must be witnessed and confirmed before the trumpet is blown to begin this feast.

Chapter 8

SEVEN REASONS FOR A POST-TRIB RAPTURE

Let's begin with an explanation of what the Pre-Trib Rapture, Mid-Trib Rapture, Pre-Wrath Rapture, and Post-Trib Rapture views are. By rapture, I mean the time when God's elect are caught up to be with the Lord in the air.

The Pre-Trib Rapture view claims the church will be raptured before the last seven years of tribulation begins.

The Mid-Trib Rapture view places the rapture halfway through this seven-year period.

The Pre-Wrath Rapture view places the rapture two thirds of the way through the seven years when the sixth seal is opened.

The Post-Trib Rapture view claims Jesus comes back at the end the seven years at the "last trump," or the seventh trumpet judgment, and that His return is a single event with a resurrection and rapture.

These are the different views and only one can be right, so let's see which one checks out with Scripture.

Seven reasons I believe the Post-Trib view is most scriptural of the differing views.

Reason number one: Paul in his letter to the Thessalonians places the rapture after the "abomination of desolation."

Now, brethren, concerning the coming of our Lord Jesus Christ and our gathering together to Him, we ask you, not to be soon shaken in mind or troubled, either by spirit or by word or by letter, as if from us, as though the day of Christ had come. Let no one deceive you by any means; for that Day will not come unless the falling away comes first, and the man of sin is revealed, the son of perdition, who opposes and exalts himself above all that is called God or that is worshipped, so that he sits as God in the temple of God, showing himself that he is God.

(II Thessalonians 2:1-4).

This Scripture places the rapture after the Antichrist is revealed and when the "abomination of desolation" which causes a great falling away from the faith that happens 3½ years into the last seven years.

Reason number two: The rapture takes place after the mark of the beast is given:

And I saw thrones, and they sat on them, and judgment was committed to them. Then I saw the souls of those who had been beheaded for their witness to Jesus and for the word of God, who had not worshipped the beast or his image, and had not received his mark on their foreheads or on their hands. And they lived and reigned with Christ for a thousand years. But the rest of the dead did not live again until the thousand years were finished. This is the first resurrection. Blessed and holy is he who has part in the first resurrection. Over such the second death has no power, but they shall be priests of God and of Christ and shall reign with Him a thousand years (Revelation 20:4-6).

This verse clearly places the resurrection/rapture after the saints were beheaded for not taking the mark of the beast which is given out during the last 3½ years.

Reason number three: Jesus prayed for us not to be taken out of the world:

I have given them Your word; and the world has hated them because they are not of the world, just as I am not of the world. I do not pray that You should take them out of the world, but that You should keep them from the evil one. They are not of the world, just as I am not of the world. Sanctify them by Your truth. Your word is truth. As You sent Me into the world, I also have sent them into the world. And for their sakes I sanctify Myself, that they also may be sanctified by the truth. I do not pray for these alone, but also for those who will believe in Me through their word.

(John 17:14-20).

Jesus included those who would believe in Him through the apostle's word and that means us. Jesus prayed that His followers would not be taken out of the world, but that we would be sent into the world to be a witness of His mighty power at this time. Jesus, also, prayed for protection for us, not evacuation. Jesus has a job for His church to do during Daniel's 70th week, and He is preparing us today for this.

Reason number four: God's people bring Him glory when they stand up against evil, not by escaping from it:

Precious in the sight of the Lord is the death of His saints (Psalm 116:15).

When Steven was martyred, Jesus honored him by standing up to receive him into heaven. Paul was later converted because of Steven's witness. Many will be saved because of the witness of the Christians that respond in a godly way when they go through persecution. I personally know of people today who were saved because they saw Christians who were being mistreated respond in a godly way.

Reason number five: To escape trials and tribulation is not consistent with the way God has done things in the past.

God allowed the first century Christians to suffer to test their faith and they were not appointed to wrath. God has used adversity to mature His saints in the past and I am sure He will continue to do this. He is coming back for a bride without spot or wrinkle, and it will be the Great Tribulation that will make her ready:

And not only that, but we also glory in tribulations, knowing that tribulation produces perseverance and perseverance, character; and character, hope Now hope does not disappoint, because the love of God has been poured out in our hearts by the Holy Spirit who was given to us (Romans 5:3-5)

Before I was afflicted, I went astray, but now I keep Your word (Psalm 119:67).

Therefore, since Christ suffered for us in the flesh, arm yourselves also with the same mind, for he who has suffered in the flesh has ceased from sin (I Peter 4:1).

These Scriptures make it clear how God still uses trials and suffering to clean us up and to grow us up. It is the refiner's fire.

Reason number six: The understanding of what the "wrath of God" is and when it begins:

And the kings of the earth, the great men, the rich men, the commanders, the mighty men, every slave and every free man, hid themselves in the caves and in the rocks of the mountains, and said to the mountains and rocks, "Fall on us and hide us from the face of Him who sits on the throne and from the wrath of the Lamb! For the great day of His wrath has come, and who is able to stand?" (Revelation 6:15-17).

At the opening of the sixth seal the "wrath of God" is announced and by this time we are well into the Great Tribulation. The "wrath of God" begins with the opening of the seventh seal and the sounding of the first trumpet judgment and ends with the last bowl judgment. Jesus returns at the seventh trumpet judgment; the church is resurrected/raptured at that time and then the bowl judgments are poured out after the seven years are completed:

Then a third angel followed them, saying with a loud voice, "If anyone worships the beast and his image, and receives his mark on his forehead or on his hand, he himself shall also drink of the wine of the wrath of God, which is poured out full strength into the cup of His indignation. He shall be tormented with fire and brimstone in the presence of the holy angels and in the presence of the Lamb (Revelation 14:9-10).

Believers are "not appointed to wrath" but our faith will be tested by fire as the first century Christians were. The only people that will experience the "wrath of God" are the ones who take the mark of the beast.

The mark of the beast is not given until the last part of Daniel's 70th week.

God can keep His people from experiencing His wrath while they are still here too like He did for the Israelites who were in Goshen not experiencing the plagues. So, it is possible to be in the world while the "wrath of God" is being poured out and be protected.

A thousand may fall at your side, and ten thousand at your right hand; But it shall not come near you. Only with your eyes shall you look and see the reward of the wicked (Psalm 91:7-8).

The danger in believing in the Pre-Trib Rapture is that those who believe they are going to be raptured before the Great Tribulation will be disillusioned and confused when they find themselves going through it. I believe many will fall away because they failed to prepare.

Reason number seven: Jesus told His disciples to pray for harvesters:

Then He said to His disciples, the harvest truly is plentiful, but the laborers are few. [38] Therefore pray the Lord of the harvest to send out laborers into His harvest" (Matthew 9:37-38).

Daniel's 70th week is God's final harvest. There are so many saved during Daniel's 70th week, no one can count them (Revelation 7:9). You don't bring your workers home during harvest time because they are needed in the fields. During the harvest everyone works.

Many Christians will be preaching the gospel, healing the sick, raising the dead and other signs and wonders following that will open the eyes of many to the gospel.

These are my reasons for believing in a Post-Trib Rapture. I don't see a two-stage return of the Lord. I see us going up to meet the Lord and being gathered to Him and then ushering Him back to earth to help Him set up His millennial reign.

Chapter 9

APPLICATION

Understanding what God is doing to close out this age is important but if it doesn't give the desire to prepare, it is useless.

So, what should we do?

Spend more time seeking a closer relationship with the Lord through reading His word, spending more time in prayer and fasting. It is also important to stay in fellowship with like-minded believers:

Therefore, brethren, having boldness to enter the Holiest by the blood of Jesus, by a new and living way which He consecrated for us, through the veil, that is, His flesh, and having a High Priest over the house of God, let us draw near with a true heart in full assurance of faith, having our hearts sprinkled from an evil conscience and our bodies washed with pure water. Let us hold fast the confession of our hope without wavering, for He who promised is faithful. And let us consider one another in order to stir up love and good works, not forsaking the assembling of ourselves together, as is the manner of some, but exhorting one another, and so much the more as you see the Day approaching. (Hebrews 10:19-25)

We should start preparing spiritually, mentally and physically for what is coming and have understanding of what God is doing so we can keep our hearts soft by being fast to forgive and we need to learn to love our enemies. It will important to know that no matter what we are called to endure, it is for our ultimate good. The world will be offended and angry with God and the Christians and those who believed in a Pre-Trib rapture and don't understand what God is doing could be deceived and take the mark of the beast.

Those who do wickedly against the covenant he (Antichrist)) shall corrupt with flattery; but the people who know their God shall be strong, and carry out great exploits. And those of the people who understand shall instruct many; yet for many days they shall fall by sword and flame, by captivity and plundering. (Daniel11:32-33)

We can start prayer groups calling out for mercy.

"Now, therefore," says the Lord, "Turn to Me with all your heart, with fasting, with weeping, and with mourning." So, rend your heart, and not your garments; return to the Lord your God, for He is gracious and merciful, slow to anger, and of great kindness; and He relents from doing harm. Who knows if He will turn and relent, and leave a blessing behind Him— A grain offering and a drink offering for the Lord your God? (Joel 2:12-14)

Our God is good and there will be pockets of refuge for those who are praying now and calling out for mercy.

The church needs to get ready to bring in a big harvest. Pray for laborers to be sent into the harvest.

The church needs to return to the example given to us by God through the first century church. Over the years man's attempt to control man has crept into the church and has polluted it. It has led to a division between believers and clergy which in not scriptural because of the priesthood of all believers. Godly leadership is leading by example and not by controlling others. The first century church had leadership shared among elders with no one exalting themselves over another. We need to get back to the Bible.

Let's get back to what works!

CONCLUSION

Paul, the apostle, puts things in perspective for us:

Though I speak with the tongues of men and of angels, but have not love, I have become sounding brass or a clanging cymbal. And though I have the gift of prophecy, and understand all mysteries and all knowledge, and though I have all faith, so that I could remove mountains, but have not love, I am nothing. And though I bestow all my goods to feed the poor, and though I give my body to be burned, but have not love, it profits me nothing (1 Corinthians 13:1-4).

It is important to know the end-times prophecies and what God is doing today, but Paul tells us that walking is love is the most important thing we can do, and Jesus warns us that when persecution comes the love of many will grow cold.

Then they will deliver you up to tribulation and kill you, and you will be hated by all nations for My name's sake. And then many will be offended, will betray one another, and will hate one another. Then many false prophets will rise up and deceive many. And because lawlessness will abound, the love of many will grow cold. But he who endures to the end shall be saved. And this gospel of the kingdom will be preached in all the world as a witness to all the nations, and then the end will come (Matthew 24:9-14).

The most important thing we can do is not to become bitter and to keep our hearts soft and then we will make it through what is coming.

My prayer for you is to keep your eyes on Jesus to make it through the coming days. It is a race, and though at times it may seem like a marathon, be of good cheer, because you can do all things through

Christ who strengthens you and remember:

Blessed be the God and Father of our Lord Jesus Christ, the Father of mercies and God of all comfort, who comforts us in all our tribulation, that we may be able to comfort those who are in any trouble, with the comfort with which we ourselves are comforted by God (2 Corinthians 1:3-4).

Let's be pressing into the Holy Spirit to get the comfort we need in times of trouble so that we can comfort others and be encouraged because Jesus is sitting at the right hand of God making intercession for us.

The End

APPENDIX

CHART OF SEALS, TRUMPETS, AND BOWLS

Second Coming

Seals	Seals	Bowl Judgments
1 2 3 4	5 6 7	1 2 3 4 5 6 7
World Experiencing: Deception War Famine God's People Experiencing: Revival Great commission Fulfilled. $3^{1/2}$ Years	World Experiencing Pestilence Cosmic signs Trumpets Last year God's People Experiencing: Martyrdom Great Tribulation Two Witnesses 1260 Days $3^{1/2}$ Years	They fall after Great Tribulation and before millennial reign begins. (Daniel 12:11-12)

A covenant with many that ushers in the last seven years (Daniel 9:27). The "abomination of desolation," is set up in the middle of the seven years and Jesus returns and resurrects and raptures His elect at the end of it.

www.ingramcontent.com/pod-product-compliance
Lightning Source LLC
Chambersburg PA
CBHW052121030426
42335CB00025B/3081

* 9 7 8 1 9 7 0 2 8 3 3 0 3 *